Ask Anna

Ask Anna

ADVICE FOR THE
FURRY AND FORLORN

WITHDRAWN

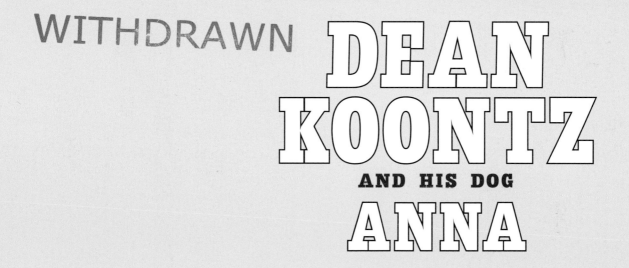

DEAN KOONTZ
AND HIS DOG
ANNA

PHOTOGRAPHY BY
VINCENT REMINI

CENTER STREET

New York

Nashville

Boston

Acknowledgments

I, Anna Koontz, dog, wish to thank the many troubled tail waggers who came to me for advice, because without them, there would have been no book. On the other hand, without them, there would have been more time for tummy rubs, tug-toy games, tennis-ball chasing, and long, interesting sessions of sniffing around the yard and through the shrubbery. Oh, well, when one has the Dear Abby gene, helping others stand strongly on their own four feet is more rewarding than just about anything but sausage. Except for me, my buddy Jackson, and my buddy Buddy, all the dogs in this book appear herein under false names to ensure their confidentiality. Some have worn disguises. Others have attempted to alter their appearances by assuming uncharacteristic expressions.

Center Street / Hachette Book Group
1290 Avenue of the Americas
New York, NY 10104

www.CenterStreet.com

Printed in the United States of America
WOR

Originally printed in hardcover by Hachette Book Group
First trade edition: October 2015
10 9 8 7 6 5 4 3 2 1

Center Street is a division of Hachette Book Group, Inc. The Center Street name and logo are trademarks of Hachette Book Group, Inc.

The Hachette Speakers Bureau provides a wide range of authors for speaking events. To find out more, go to www.HachetteSpeakersBureau.com or call 866-376-6591.

The publisher is not responsible for websites (or their content) that are not owned by the publisher.

ISBN: 9781455530809 (PBK.)

COPYRIGHT © 2014 BY DEAN KOONTZ

ALL PHOTOGRAPHS BY VINCENT REMINI

BOOK DESIGN BY MICHAEL HENTGES
AFTER AN ORIGINAL DESIGN BY TINA TAYLOR

To all my friends at Canine Companions for Independence.
You formed me into the good dog that I have become.
My rare naughtiness is entirely to my discredit.
—*Anna*

For the longest time,

I didn't realize that our dog, Anna, had the Dear Abby gene. I frequently observed her in what I could have sworn were urgent, whispered conversations with other dogs in the neighborhood. At risk of bee stings and skunk assaults and worse, I stealthily crept up on them, from bush to tree to bush, but again and again, when I got near enough to hear, they were always just panting or snorting or making other meaningless doggie sounds. I became suspicious that Anna was involved in some clandestine canine political movement aimed at getting better-tasting treats and putting an end to the leash laws. Golden Retrievers are known for their go-along-to-get-along sweetness, but they're also known for their keen intelligence, and I thought perhaps she could justify deceiving me if the cause was important enough.

Eventually, I became aware that she appeared to be having whispered conversations with all sorts of people we encountered in our daily life: the mailman, the FedEx guy, the neighbors, the fellow who washes the windows, various landscapers, the repairman who came to fix our electronic high-speed wafflemaker... With stealth that any sneak thief would envy, I slyly crept up on them, but repeatedly I found, as before, that Anna and her companions were just panting and snorting and making other meaningless doggie sounds. I remained suspicious, and when I saw the pool guy on his knees weeping with gratitude, while with one paw Anna patted him on the shoulder as if to say, "There, there," I knew that something must be afoot.

Proof came when I discovered that Anna had secretly acquired her own computer and was engaged in the dispensing of advice online to all manner of species, but mostly to other dogs. She had kept the computer concealed in our exercise room, where she knew that I would never venture. I went in there one day merely to imagine what it might be like to use the treadmill, and there she was, chatting with a troubled Boston Terrier in, of all places, Boston.

From my discussions with Anna, I understand that she concealed her advice-giving from me only because she worried that I would think her bossy, which she is not. I am proud of her, and she is proud of my Sherlockian detective work. Together we have compiled for you this book of her golden advice to other canines, with the hope that it will help you understand your dogs better and will encourage you to stop being a ninny of an owner, if in fact you are one.

—Dean Koontz

Dear Anna,
I'm little. There's a giant owl living nearby. I'm afraid to go out at night to potty, `cause he swoops down at me, and I have to *run for my life*. It's less like Disney around here, more like a Tim Burton cartoon. I'm worried the owl might figure out how to follow me through the doggy door. What should I do?

—*Muffin*

Dear Muffin,
Give me your
address. I'll be there
next Friday night.
Saturday, we'll have
owl for breakfast.
With maybe a
little cheese.
—Anna

Dear Anna,
Last Tuesday, as the wind blew me by you, I said hello, but you didn't respond. I hope your recent celebrity hasn't gone to your head. You were never stuck-up before.
—Lester

Dear Lester,
Sorry, little one. I didn't hear you speak, and I'm embarrassed to say I mistook you for a wind-tossed ball of dryer lint.
—Anna

Dear Anna,
I hope you can help me.
One neighbor has a Great Dane.
Another has an Irish Wolfhound.
I feel short. Is there anywhere I can
go for leg extensions?
   Is there some exercise I can do?
A special vitamin? Some kind
of yoga for the height challenged?

—Shrimp

Dear Shrimp,

If you measure height from tail tip to nose, you are way taller than you think. If you feel short, you will be short. If you feel tall...you'll still be short, but you'll feel better. One good thing about being a dog is we don't have to care how we look, because we're all humongously cute. Snakes should have it so good. You don't want yoga, you want yogurt, the creamy sweet frozen kind. And maybe you could go to court to have your name changed. Make them call you Big Boy or Stilts.

—Anna

Dear Anna,
Lately I have been depressed.
I am a smart dog, so the usual tug toys
and tennis balls got boring a long time
ago. Besides, I want to accomplish
something. I'm a Great Dane
mix, but I haven't been feeling
so great lately.   —Elton
What to do?

Dear Elton,

You look pretty great to me, big boy. Everybody has a talent. For instance, I'm good at giving advice, analyzing the fiction of Thomas Pynchon, and origami. Discover your talent, and you'll be happy. There used to be this pianist and comedian, Victor Borge, who called himself the Great Dane. If your talent isn't music, maybe it's painting. Or interpretive dance. Find your bliss! You're a DOG! Dogs can do anything! Except drive. Stupid traffic laws.   —Anna

Dear Anna,
I'm covered in funny spots and have what looks like a perpetual black eye. I'm afraid to ask Fifi, the Poodle on the next block, for a date, because I just know she'll turn me down. What can I do?
—Lonely in Louisiana

Dear Lonely,
      Although humans in single bars lie their heads off, dogs don't have that advantage, because dogs don't lie. However, we can imply and suggest and innocently mislead a little. Lots of girls like bad boys, so subtly imply that the Rottweiler who gave you the black eye has *two* of them. And if she's rude enough to mention the spots, just say, "It really stings when those bullets bounce off."

—*Anna*

17

Dear Anna,
You're sweet. I want to send you a box of sausages. What's the best way to get them to you?
—An Admirer in Albany

Dear Admirer,
Avoid the mailman's despicable, thieving Poodle and use either UPS or FedEx. Seal the sausages in an airtight container and label the box "catnip." Put another label on it that says, "Unauthorized opening of this package punishable by castration—this means you, Pierre." —*Anna*

Dear Anna,
I'm a Newfoundland and my sister is a Chihuahua. I love her. But how could this happen?
—Burt

Dear Burt, Although dogs are magical beings who know all the secrets of the universe and are capable of just about anything, in this case I suspect the answer is—adoption.
—Anna

Dear Anna,
I've perfected my begging technique. This gets a lot more treats than other poses I've tried. What do you think? Cool, huh?
—*Puggly*

Dear Puggly, Stop that at once. Dogs shouldn't beg. We are a noble species. We earn. We deserve. We charm, wheedle, cajole, and blandish, but we do not beg. Keep a grasp on the correct human-dog relationship. *They* beg *us*—to get in the bathtub, to swallow a pill wrapped in sliced turkey. If you beg, pretty soon they'll think that *they* allow *you* to sleep with them in the big bed. And then they'll become power-crazed.

—*Anna*

Dear Anna,
We are puppies in training with Canine
Companions for Independence, hoping to serve as
assistance dogs to people with disabilities. We know
that you went through all but two of the 24 months
of training before going to live with Dean
and Gerda Koontz. What happened?
Do you have any advice to help us avoid
flunking out?
—The Pups

Dear Pups,

Birds! Birds were my undoing. Don't get me
started about birds. A bunny crosses my path, and I go,
"Ho-hum, another boring rabbit." But a bird hopping across the yard,
perched in a tree, especially a bird in flight... Well, I go nuts. I chase
them, but not to catch. I want to learn the secret of flight. I could fly
if I just knew how. But will they share the secret? Will they? *Nooooooo.*
Birds are smug, haughty, conceited lords of the air. The most they'll
give you is a rude gesture with their tail feathers.

If you're tethered to a wheelchair and you drag it—with your
trainer—into a pond in pursuit of a duck, you're out of the program.
If, while chasing a crow, you drag your trainer and her wheelchair
onto a highway, off a bluff, onto train tracks, into a cornfield,
you're out, out—OUT!—of the program. It was a sad day when they
said, "Anna, you have a problem too big for us to solve."

Yes, my name is Anna, and I'm a birdaholic.

This has led to a love-hate relationship with birds. I still want to
be one—or at least a flying dog. If Dumbo, why not me? I really get
steamed by the arrogance of birds. The only revenge I get is
every Thanksgiving, when I run outside and shout at them,
"Hey, you should see what we're eatin' for dinner!" So I'm
left only with hope that this Christmas, I'll at last get the blimp
I always ask for.

Do your best, pups. That's all any of us can do. Dogs always try
to do their best. Cats? Not so much. Birds? Hey, don't get me started
about birds! Alfred Hitchcock had it right. Never trust a bird!

Never, never! But, ah, to fly.

As ever,

—*Anna*

Dear Anna,
When I turn my ears just so, I can see the future.
The cars will drive themselves but only where Google wants
them to go. If someone signs up as a friend and you don't like him,
Facebook will whack him for $15,000. A McDonald's Happy Meal
will one day cost $3,299. The superhero movies will keep
getting dumber, and 90-year-old rap artists on tour
eventually won't be able to remember the lyrics
and invent a craze called "gibberish rap."
—*Nostradamus*

28

Dear Nos,
Never mind all that. Will dogs ever be elected to the presidency and the congress? Or will we continue to be ruled by the dumbest humans among us?
        —Anna

Dear Anna,
When my human mom and dad go out to dinner, I miss them terribly. I lie in my bed, in the throes of melancholy, tortured by anxiety, alert for the first sound of them. What if they have a flat tire?
What if they're carjacked?
What if they're in an accident?
—Worried in Wauwatosa

Dear Worried in Wauwatosa,
What if they're eating cheeseburgers?
What if they're eating steaks?
What if they're eating nachos?
—Anna

Dear Anna,
My owner thinks it's totally funny when he says, "Shake," and I raise my paw, and then he won't shake, and I'm left just sort of hanging there. What's wrong with him?
—Brownie

Dear Brownie,
He's an idiot. There are two ways to deal with him. First, be even sweeter than usual, cuddlier and lickier and cuter and more loving, until you make him feel like a swine. Or second, try a little tough love combined with Pavlovian training: Each time he pulls this stunt, pee on his shoes. I recommend the former, but I would personally delight in the latter. —Anna

Dear Anna,
I'm concerned that I'm not cute enough. Dogs have to be supercute at *all* times or nobody wants them. I'll be given to the pound if I'm not cute enough. And I'm *not!* I'm not cute enough! I know all of this because the family cat told me so.
The family cat knows everything. He is a genius!
—*Not Cute Enough in Cleveland*

Dear Cute Enough,
You've often heard the old saying, "All dogs go to Heaven." I'll bet my tail you've never heard "All cats go to Heaven." Maybe some cats might, but not all. Because some cats lie. They lie, they deceive, they sneak, and they potty in a box in the house! Their breath smells like fish-based pet food and dead mice. If any animal in your home has a cuteness deficit, it isn't you!

—Anna

35

Dear Anna,
My human parents think my big tongue is funny. They make jokes about my big funny tongue. I don't think it's funny. I think their furless faces are funny, and the way they walk around on two legs is *hysterical*. But I don't think my tongue is funny. Do you think my tongue is funny?
—*Object of Mockery*

Dear Object,
Your tongue is not funny. The ideal tongue length is approximately the length of your ear, as are yours and mine. The average human tongue is half again as long as the human ear. Therefore, as far as tongues are concerned, every human being is as deformed as the Hunchback of Notre Dame, but *we* don't mock *them*. Another thing they don't understand about tongues: life is short, and there's so much that needs to be licked!
—*Anna*

Dear Anna,
I love New York City!
My favorite places
are Central Park and
the pool in Washington
Square! What's
your favorite place
in New York?
—Otto

Dear Otto,
The Metropolitan Museum of Art, second floor, European paintings, especially the Dutch, Italian, and Flemish galleries. I could spend hours studying Van Dyck's painting, *James Stuart, Duke of Richmond and Lennox.*
—Anna

Dear Anna,
I'm gonna chew my way out of this prison. I've had enough of this stinkin' place—the poached chicken breast, the fancy cookies, the occasional banana with peanut butter, fresh water whenever I want it, the toys, the tummy rubs, the long cuddles on the sofa, the sweet talk. I want to run wild. I want to drink from the gutter and fight under the moon and terrify smaller animals.
—Sylvester

Dear Sylvester,
You listen to me, mister, *and you listen good.* You're talking like a cat, and I will have none of it. You're a dog, and you will act like a dog. Nobody wants to hear your trash talk. Stop embarrassing your species, straighten up, and start waggin' in gratitude for being born a dog.
—*Anna*

Dear Anna,
What is it about tennis balls? Huh? What is it? Why do we like to chase after them and chase after them until we *exhaust* ourselves?

There's something so alluring about them, so enchanting, but we can't quite define their attraction. *Our new ones squeak!* They didn't use to squeak, but now they squeak! What is it about them? Huh? What is it? What is it?

—Mutt and Jeff

Dear Mutt and Jeff, Tennis balls are mystical objects symbolizing the perfect roundness of creation, reminding us that life is a chase toward our destiny. Each tennis ball is a symbol of eternal joy and eternal life. Humans bat them away with rackets because, sadly, humans are afraid to bite the concept of eternity and chew it. *Mine squeaks, too!!!*

—Anna

Dear Anna,
Every time I'm left alone on the front seat of a vehicle, I am tempted to drive. I hope I can, I think I can, I *know* I can, even though I have been discouraged from doing so by the clerk at the DMV, who wouldn't accept my application for a learner's permit. Nevertheless, I am tempted. Am I a bad dog? —*Speedy*

Dear Speedy,
No. You are just ambitious and inspired. As men once walked on the moon, so dogs will one day drive. Though it's difficult to drive well with your head out the window.
—Anna

Dear Anna,
I'm always chewing things. Chew, chew, chew. Shoelaces, insoles, sofa legs, chair legs, rugs, lamp cord— A sudden *zzzzzing!* followed by darkness and a dream in which I'm reincarnated as a Petco store manager with an all-you-can-eat privilege in the dog-treat aisle.

Then *fisssspip*, I wake to find myself twenty feet from the lamp, hanging from the ceiling by my claws. Chew, chew, chew. Rubber doorstop, slippers, draperies. What's wrong with me?
—*Obsessed in Omaha*

Dear Obsessed,
    Maybe you've chewed one too many lamp cords. Otherwise, don't worry. You're a puppy. You'll outgrow it. Just in case you're a slow learner— never try to fish a stuck English muffin out of a toaster with a fork.
                    —Anna

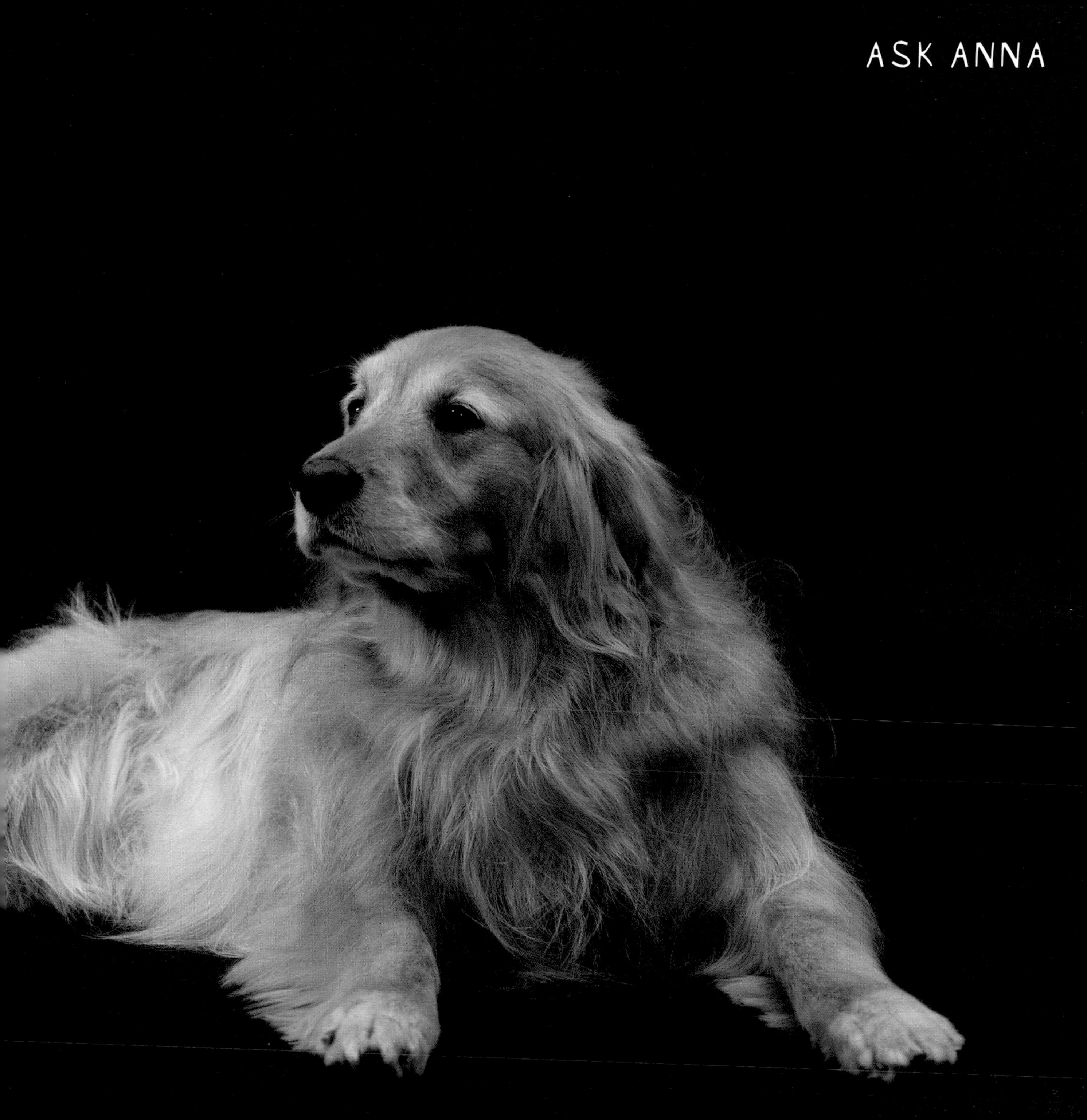
ASK ANNA

Dear Anna, I am a Bernese Mountain Dog. We were first bred in the Berne district of Switzerland. We were developed as draft animals. Our ancestors pulled carts for cheesemakers and weavers. I love my family, but we live in Palm Beach, Florida. No mountains. No weavers. No cheesemakers. I feel...displaced. What should I do? —Fritz

Dear Fritz, What you should do every morning is thank God you're not wading through deep snow, pulling a cart laden with cheeses that REALLY STINK and with some 200-pound cheesemaker half insane due to the low oxygen content of air in the Alps, yodeling till he makes your ears bleed. Be a free spirit! Embrace the whole spectrum of fun dog behavior. Run on the beach, like a Golden Retriever! Swim in the warm ocean, like a Labrador! Run in circles and jump about for no reason, like a Jack Russell terrier! —Anna

A Brief History of Canine Advice

One of the best-kept secrets throughout history has been the role that the wise advice of dogs has played in human affairs. Over centuries, many of the most successful and celebrated individuals who secured their place in the annals of humankind would have been forgotten losers if they had failed to heed the counsel of their dogs. For instance, misunderstanding the word "ark", Noah at first thought that God required him to build a gigantic wooden arc, whereupon he spent weeks constructing the lamentably primitive equivalent of the Gateway Arch in Saint Louis, Missouri, which he intended to paint in the colors of the rainbow, with a big smiley face at the apex. Thanks to the patient, gentle admonitions of his dog, Fluffy, Noah one day looked up at the arch, did a double take, smacked his forehead with the palm of one hand, said, "Idiot!" and hurriedly got to work on a humongous boat.

In the third century B.C., the Carthaginian general Hannibal crossed the Alps and invaded Italy in the Second Punic War. His success, due in no small part to the use of armored elephants, could have been a monumental embarrassment if he had proceeded with his first choice, armored giraffes wearing berets. Even his second choice—hordes of unarmored but extremely annoying monkeys bashing together pairs of cymbals—would undoubtedly have been a military catastrophe. Fortunately, his dog, Spike, aware that his master was too prideful ever to heed the advice of a canine, waited until the fabled general fell asleep; then, night after night, he whispered in the great man's ear, "Elephants . . . elephants . . ."

In the year 1000, the Indian mathematician Sridhara was the first to recognize the importance of the zero, leading not only to rapid advancements in all of the sciences but also to shrewder pricing of items in supermarkets. Prior to this, Sridhara had stubbornly held to the belief that the most important of all numbers was three, except on alternate Wednesdays, when obviously it was five. We need not belabor here the source of his enlightenment. Her name was Furball.

In 1014, Sweyn Forkbeard, a Viking king, died unexpectedly in Gainsborough, England, and was succeeded by his young son, Canute. Canute at once fled to Denmark because Ethelred returned from Normandy to rule the English. Only one in 20 million people has ever heard of any of these men because none of them had a dog.

In 1335, in Japan, the private army of the Hojo family attempted to depose Emperor Godaigo. A warlord named Ashikaga supported Godaigo, and the Hojo forces were crushed. Historians long ago established beyond doubt that Godaigo and Ashikaga had dogs and that the Hojos had cats.

One admirer of Vermeer's 17th-century art has said that the paint seems to have floated invisibly onto the canvas, like snow, and then melted into it. But as modern technology has allowed high-resolution studies of *Girl With the Red Hat*, the fine silky strokes of a dog's tail hairs—most likely an ancestor of the modern-day Golden Retriever—are visible in several key details of what is arguably the finest masterpiece by this greatest of all painters.

Mozart's Pompom, Proust's Madeleine, Churchill's Reggie, Einstein's Emcee, and so many others: Would it be an exaggeration to claim that without the advice of dogs at critical points in the advance of civilization, our world would be one vast and terrible totalitarian megastate without human rights, mired in medieval poverty and ignorance, awash in wretched and undanceable music, bespoiled by art that celebrated ugliness instead of beauty, its library shelves groaning with unreadable literature despised by even the illiterate masses? No. No, it would not be an exaggeration to make this claim. If anything, such a claim would be an understatement, inadequate to properly depict a world where the advice of dogs had never been heeded.

I tell you, Jackson, your small bones are aerodynamic, your high fluff factor will provide lift, and if you pass gas at exactly the right moment, you'll be airborne.
Yeah, but Toto flew only 'cause he got caught in a tornado.

One small step for a dog, one giant leap for dogkind!

Dear Anna,
Sometimes when I'm sniffing the ground, I step on my ears. It's embarrassing. What should I do?
—Huckleberry

Dear Huckleberry,
Do what any cat does when
falling off a window sill: Pretend
the dumb move was intentional.
—Anna

Dear Anna,
My friend Pepper and I like to play fight, but her bad breath is beyond hideous, so the play is no fun. How do I tell her without hurting her feelings? —Salt

Dear Salt,

The problem is not Pepper but her owner, who is not performing proper dental hygiene on her. In Pepper's company, with your tube of doggie toothpaste in your mouth, go to her owner. If the owner misunderstands and brushes *your* teeth, endure it. Then make a big deal out of smelling Pepper's breath and pretend to vomit. If that doesn't work, my pal Buddy suggests biting the owner on the butt.

—*Anna*

Dear Anna,
I love to shred these rolls of paper. I love to unravel one through the house and then follow it back, pretending I'm with Hansel and Gretel, escaping along our marked trail through the woods, the evil witch close behind us.
I love to sneak out at night to decorate the neighbors' trees and shrubbery with one.
Is this wrong?
—*Charmin'*

Dear Charmin',
It is so right that I don't have the words to express how right it is. But please tell me you *never* drink from the toilet.
—Anna

Hey, Anna babe, No dog gets away with nothin' in my neighborhood. Know what I mean? I make the rules, and I enforce 'em. In my territory, dogs pick up their own poop in plastic bags. They bark only when barken to. Some mutt comes around here with fleas, I treat him with a concrete suit and a bath in the river. Know what I mean? It's real nice in my neighborhood. Would you like to come here and be my moll?
—Butch

Dear Butch,
I'm flattered by your expression of affection. But I must here reveal for the first time that I am a dog nun. —Anna

Dear Anna,
I live in the Big Apple.
I have to go everywhere
on a leash. In southern
California, do you have
to go everywhere on
a leash? This leash
really frustrates me.
—Miffed in Manhattan

Dear Miffed,
Your frustration will
go away as soon as you
understand that it is your
people who are leashed,
that you are walking them,
not the other way around.
When they tell you to heel
or to sit, humor them...
but just remember who
picks up whose poop.
—Anna

Dear Anna,
My intentions are entirely platonic. I greatly enjoy discussions of literature and philosophy, as I know you do as well. I would like to invite you to dinner at *Wienerschnitzel*.
Will you accept?
—*Plato*

Dear Plato,
   I'll bring the mustard.
      —*Anna*

Dear Anna,
Our names are Precious and Special. Puke. We want to be called Spike and Brute. How do we get our humans to rename us?
—Precious (gag) and Special (barf)

Dear Precious and Special,
My pal Buddy and I agree on this.
The likelihood of your being renamed
Spike and Brute is no better than
your being renamed Death and Taxes.
—Anna

Dear Anna,
You were once in training to be an assistance dog to a person with a disability, and now you write books. I would like to work, too, and earn money for treats.
What job do you think I could get?
—Cutie in Cleveland

Dear Cutie,   In the next *Stars Wars* movie, you'd make the perfect wise counselor to Jedi Knights. You've got the Look, kid. People are tired of Yoda. His syntax is all screwed up, he doesn't have fur, he looks like a wrinkled turnip with ears, he throws nasty tantrums when he's not nominated for an Oscar, and he's in Kim Kardashian's entourage, which is *soooo* yesterday.
—Anna

Dear Anna, Sometimes the cat says there's a dog trapped at the bottom of my water dish. When I look, I see a dog just like me. The cat says, "Save him! Save him!" So I try to save him from drowning, but every time I splash the water out of the dish, I can't find him in there. Could he be a dog in a parallel universe or something?
—Confused Puppy

Dear Confused,
Your problem is naivete. Think about it.
What is a synonym for "deceiver," huh? Cat.
What is a synonym for "sneaky nuisance," huh?
Cat. What is a synonym for "tormentor,"
huh? Cat. CAT, CAT, CAT, CAT!!!
By the way, there's no dog drowning
in the toilet, either.
—Anna

Dear Anna,
So, I fetch the newspaper!
I'm very proud! So happy
to be helpful that I'm walking
on air! *On air!* Then the stupid
plastic sleeve tears! The stupid,
STUPID, STUPID newspaper
comes all undone! It shreds!
My human dad spends half
the morning taping it back
together, all the while giving
me pitying looks.
Fetching the newspaper
looks easy! It's not!
It's really not! Help!
—*Frazzled in Vermont*

Dear Frazzled,
Never undergo training as a bomb-sniffing dog. As for fetching a newspaper, think of it as a duck you must retrieve for a hunter. Go for it with gusto. Grab it firmly but gently in your jaws. Hold it by the middle, not the end, as you did with the newspaper. Don't be distracted by the funny pages. Snoopy isn't doing anything that you haven't seen before. That snarky cat, Garfield, will just make you want to gag. As for the editorial pages— don't get me started.

—*Anna*

ASK ANNA

Dear Anna,
My owner's feet smell.
They really, really smell.
They stink.
—*Blackie*

Dear Blackie,
Lucky you. Savor!
—*Anna*

Dear Beauteous Miss Anna, More than a fortnight ago, by royal courier, I dispatched to you a box of the finest sausages as an expression of my admiration for your good heart, your quick mind, and your impeccable advice to those of our kind who in one way or another are lamentably afflicted. Having heard nothing from you, I correspond now to assure myself that the gift was received.

—Your Admirer, Winston

Dear Winston,
The mailman's larcenous
Poodle strikes again.
—Anna

Dear Anna,
It's me again, the Great Dane mix that you advised to overcome my depression by finding my bliss. It turns out my bliss is singing and playing the piano. But if I use my paws for the damper, una corda, and sostenuto pedals, I have nothing to play the keys with except my nose. Humans have ten fingers. I have one nose. How am I ever going to get to Carnegie Hall?
—Elton (again)

Dear Lord,
Help me with this one.
—*Anna*

Dear Anna,
We like to go to this special
dog park where we swim in dirty water,
roll in the mud, and get totally filthy.
Want to join us?
—The Little Rascals

Dear Rascals,
I have a very thick undercoat. Do you realize how long a bath would take if I got that dirty? *Two hours!* A shrieking hair dryer! I like the kind of dog park where I overlook it from a suite at the Ritz Carlton while eating chopped beef off fine china. Dogs do not have to live a cliché.
—Anna

Dear Anna,
My name is Button, which is ironic, because just this morning, as I was sniffing around my human Mom's sewing room, I saw this shiny blue button on the floor, and without thinking, I ate it.
I'm a little scared that eating it will hurt me.
What should I do?
—Button

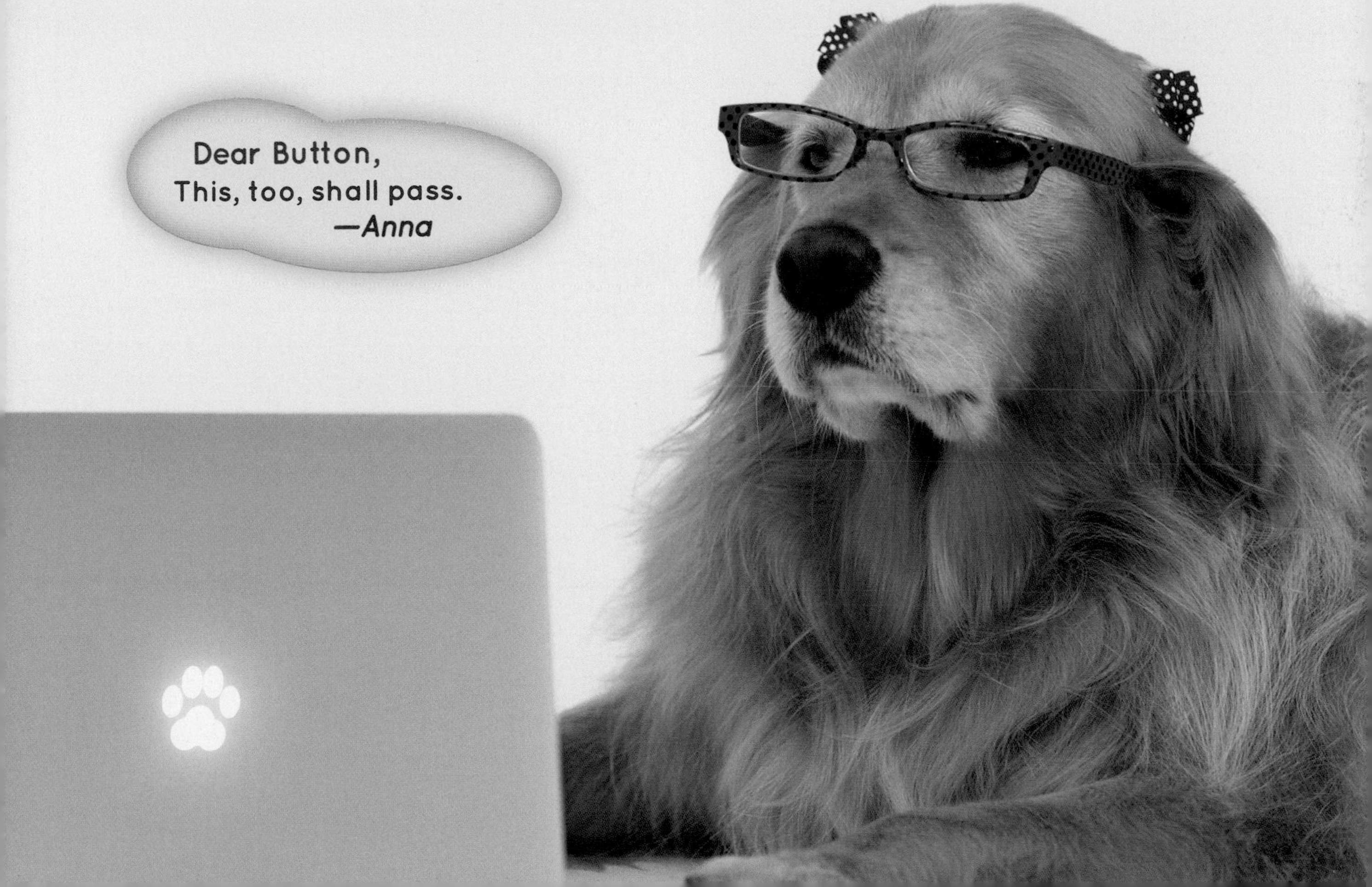
Dear Button,
This, too, shall pass.
—Anna

Dear Anna,
Everyone thinks I'm a tough guy because of my mug and the way I'm built. I'm not a tough guy. I'm sensitive. I can be tender. I have deep feelings. Every time I see *Steel Magnolias*, I cry. It's a flood. What can I do to convince people I'm not a tough guy?
—*Misunderstood*

Dear Misunderstood,
No one will think you're a tough guy if you just keep wearing that tube top, halter top, whatever the freakin' thing is.
—Anna

Dear Anna,
    I'm told that I sit on my post so that all the huge and powerful dogs in this class can be trained not to be distracted by me. I think the truth is, they're being trained not to eat small dogs. What if one of them doesn't learn the lesson?
    —Bite-size

Dear Bite-size,
Then good-bye, so long,
farewell, amen.
—Anna

Dear Anna,
Do you ever worry about the human race?
They're always rushing pell-mell
toward one cliff or another.
I worry about them a lot.
—Worrywort in Waikiki

Dear Worrywort,
How can you not worry about a species that won't always give a dog sofa privileges, that thinks tacos are only human food, that saves our poop in little bags—to what possible purpose? —and that built nuclear bombs?
But you gotta love them. Love is the only thing that will save them. *—Anna*

A Dog Day in Koontzland

We live in dangerous and stressful times, more terrible even than the era when human beings were hunted by slavering packs of sabre-toothed tigers the size of Buicks and by flocks of flying monkeys with malevolent intent. The unprecedented danger and stressfulness of our blighted time is in fact confirmed by the Federal Office of Danger and Stress Measurement, by the United States Department of Danger and Stress Containment, and by the Bureau of Look Out the Sky Is Falling. None of us is ever truly safe, neither a well-known writer like me, Dean Koontz, nor an obscure and struggling actor like that Ben Affleck guy I saw reciting Shakespeare's sonnets on a street corner in return for the coins with which passersby pelted him.

What seems to be an ordinary day when we wake up can suddenly become a fearsome day of vicious strife and desperate struggle, of seething deceit and blistering treachery, of mortal encounters with shrieking maniacs in a doughnut shop. One moment we can be serene, even blissful, but just an instant later, we might find ourselves the target of an enraged shoe-store clerk, plunged waist-deep in a muck of confusion and horror, swept away by towering tsunamis of delusion, when we can't tell the difference between truth and lies, when we don't know whether we're coming or going, or whether we've come and gone and come back again, when we don't know what's up and what's down and what's just floating out there between up and down, floating like a wispy ball of cotton candy that could be harmless or that could be the equivalent of Darth Vader's Death Star.

Worse, our potential assailants aren't limited to other human beings, because Mother Nature operates a madhouse populated with homicidal creatures that want only to eat us, with or without an appropriate beverage. If you swore to provide a crocodile with a lifetime supply of Big Macs and fries, if the beast patiently and fairly considered your proposition, arriving at the most reasonable conclusion that your offer was generous, indeed a culinary bonanza, it would nonetheless forgo McDonald's Happy Meals and devour you alive, without benefit of pickles or special sauce. I once knew of a grizzly bear that much preferred dark chocolate to human flesh, but then it developed diabetes and returned to a diet of forest-service personnel.

I am in a grim but determined mood when I now direct your attention to the fact that those animals that *don't* eat human beings will nevertheless, from time to time, be possessed by the urge to kill us. Cows suddenly stampede, trampling anyone in their way, even women and children, even well-meaning members of the National Society for Charity to Cows.

Why? Why are bears and crocodiles and cows and countless other animals such ruthless killing machines? I can't explain. That is a timeless mystery for the greatest philosophers to probe with all of the dedication of a urologist performing a prostate exam. Both Plato and Aristotle struggled unsuccessfully with the question. Perhaps one day our most esteemed contemporary philosopher, Adam Sandler, will achieve the explanatory insight.

Anyway, my contention is that the worst thugs in the animal kingdom wish to kill us *because they envy us*. They can't get a good table at a fancy restaurant. We can. Regardless of their age, they can't buy beer, wine, or other adult drinks. We can. They never put one of their own on the moon, and they never will. We did. Envy is a terrible thing. It leads to bitterness, hatred, even murder. A little bluejay is no more immune to envy than is a crocodile yearning for a fine cabernet sauvignon, which is most likely why birds so often dive-bomb me.

And what about microbes? Bacteria and viruses are too small to have brains, yet they act as if the whole purpose of their existence is to sicken and kill us. I could wake up one morning to a warm, glorious California day, the sea spangled with sunlight, the graceful palms swaying in a gentle breeze, our singular politicians working gallantly in Sacramento to repeal reality—and then much to my surprise and dismay, the industrious activities of despicable and lawless microbes could be revealed at breakfast, when my nose comes loose and falls into my cereal. It could happen. And much worse.

The threats we face in these dangerous and stressful times are innumerable, especially for those of us who never quite got the hang of mathematics. Earthquakes, mud slides, tornadoes, hurricanes, volcanic eruptions, runaway trucks under the influence of demonic spirits, lava lamps in which the shape-changing mass is actually an evil alien waiting for us to fall asleep, suspicious molds and an even more suspicious fungus, the children's-party clown whose main act proves to be juggling the birthday boy or girl along with two running chain saws: It is a miracle that we aren't all hopelessly neurotic and in the iron grip of fear.

Most of you *are* hopelessly neurotic and in the iron—or at least aluminum—grip of fear, but you could join the rest of us who have escaped that pitiable condition. All you need is a dog for a companion. Dogs are unique in all of nature, unfailingly humble and faithful and without envy. We all know "dog" is "God" spelled backward, which is more worth considering than that "golf" is "flog" spelled backward or that the syllables of the words "ham sandwich" are, in the language of ancient Babylonia, an obscene suggestion involving figs.

Dogs possess the innocence and many of the virtues of angels, and I suspect that most of them are more assured of a place in Heaven than I am. On a bad day in Koontzland, when my handcrafted jet pack takes me head-on into a tree, when an IRS auditor shows up to question that $67,000 deduction for tiny pickled ears of corn and other business-lunch condiments, when my investment in that alternative-energy lunar-power company is threatened by the shocking discovery that the moon is often not fully lit, I need only hold my dog's paw or rub her behind the ears, or let her rub me behind the ears, or smooth the soft white fur on her belly, and all my troubles melt away like a strawberry-flavored tab of antipsychotic medication dissolving under the tongue. Anna—in fact any dog—is not only a source of good advice but also a bridge over troubled waters, and not only a bridge but a 12-lane causeway.

Woof.